"HARRY'S BIRD"

by

Tony Breeze

CHARACTERS

Harry Moss.........   middle-aged, intelligent but very bitter

Moira.............   Harry's wife, of similar age but unable to relate to him because of some past trauma

Sister McCluskey....   Quietly efficient nurse who distances herself in order to preserve her sanity

Debbie.............   Sixteen year old tearaway from the Probation Hostel next door who's been in trouble all her life

(Interior and exterior views of large Victorian house – front door, hallway, reception desk, staircase with chairlift leading to upper bedroom (or ramp to indicate upper room) – outside there's a patio with walled garden...the song entitled "Harry" is played ...we hear a taxi arrive, its door slam and as it drives off in comes Harry carrying a suitcase while his wife tries to take it from him. He is obviously unwell but putting on a brave front)

Moira   Here, let me help you

Harry   I can manage, I'm not completely useless

Moira   Have it your own way

           (She is about to ring the bell)

Harry   Wait – I want to look at it

Moira   What for ?

Harry   I want to remember what it looks like – from the outside ... O.K. ring the bell

           (She does so and a woman appears in neat clothes wearing a badge)

Sister M   Mr Moss ?

Harry   (Sarcastically) Is this the Seaview Guest House ?

Moira   Ignore him – its his idea of a joke

Harry	We've booked a double room overlooking the sea - with single beds of course
Sister	Come in
Harry	Do I have to ?
Moira	Go on
	(They enter)
Harry	You might have the wrong name - can you check your records ?
Sister	(Checking book) <u>Harry</u> Moss ?
Harry	Damn, they got me again
Sister	You must be Mrs Moss
Harry	(Indicating nurse) She's good isnt she ? (To nurse) Have you ever thought of becoming a police woman ?
Sister	I cant say I have
Harry	Instead of a nurse - you are a nurse I presume ?
Sister	Yes, we dont wear uniform
Harry	I see - low profile - (confidentially) How do they know then who's who ?
Sister	The badge
Harry	I see (He peers close to read it) Sister...

Sister	McCluskey (Offers her hand) Pleased to meet you
Harry	(Ignoring it) Would you be awfully offended Sister if I dont reciprocate the sentiment on this occasion — I'm sure under normal circumstances you're a simply wonderful person but you'll know what I mean when I say that at this particular moment I wish we'd never actually met
Sister	(Unperturbed shaking hands with Moira) Mrs Moss
Harry	Whats the procedure then ? Do I have to register ? Leave my gold teeth with reception ?
Sister	Have you got any valuables ?
Harry	The only thing I value now is time
Sister	Yes — well we can sort out the details later — would you like to see your room ?
Harry	(Falsely) That would be nice
Sister	This way — you can leave your case till later
Harry	Thats all right, I can manage
	(They go towards the stairs)
	It doesnt look like a hospice
Sister	Doesnt it ? What does it look like ?
Harry	I dont know, I imagined echoing corridors and the smell of disinfectant

Sister	We try to make it as homely as possible
Harry	Thus the lack of uniforms
Sister	You found us all right then ?
Harry	Unfortunately yes
Moira	We took a taxi
Harry	(Sarcastically) We dont normally run to taxis but this was a special occasion
Sister	This is your room
Moira	Its nice Harry
Harry	Wonderful - and this is the bed
Moira	(Sitting on it) Its very comfortable
Harry	I often wondered where I'd spend my last days - you should have a plaque up you know - "Harry Moss slept here" - or perhaps "slept" isnt the right verb
Sister	I'm sure you'll be quite comfortable
Moira	I'm sure he will
Harry	"Comfortable ?" Are you sure thats the right word Sister?
Sister	We do our best to make everything as "comfortable" as possible
Harry	Thats fine then, simply spiffing
Sister	If you'd like to unpack

Moira	Can I have a word with you nurse ?
Sister	Of course
	(They go outside)
Moira	I'm worried about him
Sister	Naturally
Moira	No, I mean his attitude - he's gone so insular - saying things - things that are hurtful - he didnt used to be like this - I suppose I want to apologise for him in advance as it were
Sister	Dont worry Mrs Moss, we're quite used to it
Moira	If he should offend somebody will you tell them, will you explain - he's not normally like this
Sister	It isnt a normal situation though is it ?
Moira	No, I suppose not
Sister	I'll put the kettle on
Harry	(As Moira returns) What was all that about ?
Moira	Nothing
Harry	Come off it, you dont talk about nothing - what were you doing , talking about me ?
Moira	Apologising for your manners if you must know
Harry	You dont have to - you're not answerable for what I do

Moira	Harry, why do you have to be so hurtful ? Its hard enough as it is
Harry	(With venom) Its hard for you is it ? Having a husband who's on the way out - well how do you think it feels for the bloody husband ?1
Moira	If only you'd think before you speak
Harry	I've done my share of thinking - caring about other people - look where it got me... I think you'd better go
Moira	Bye then (She approaches him to kiss goodbye - there is a moments hesitation because of the psychological gap between them) I'll see you tomorrow
Harry	You wont - if you think I'm putting up with you every day you've got another thing coming - you can come every other day and once on Sundays
Moira	They dont mind visitors
Harry	No, but I do
Moira	I'll pray for you Harry
Harry	You wont - if you so much as say one Hail Mary that will be it - its not too late for a divorce you know
Moira	If only you'd try to believe, it'd be such a weight off your mind
Harry	It would, wouldnt it - all the problems handed over to "He who knows everything" - I could walk round then with one of those silly

grins all over my face like your Christian friends

Moira It helps

Harry Not to me it doesnt - I stopped believing in God the same time I stopped believing in Santa Claus

Moira Its burning you up Harry

Harry (Pointedly) No love, the burning comes later

   (She is upset and turns to go as the nurse arrives with two cups of tea)

Sister Arent you staying for a cuppa Mrs Moss ?

Moira I'd better be going - its all right, I can see myself out

   (She exits tearfully)

Sister She's very upset

Harry What do you expect ? She's leaving her husband to waste away in a hospice bed

Sister Do you enjoy it Mr Moss ?

Harry What ?

Sister Making your wife suffer - its hard enough as it is for the relatives

Harry Oh she loves it really - she'll be there at church tonight - "Please God, make Harry better" - and then when it doesnt work - "Ah

well, it must have been Gods will" - nice
really - either way she cant lose

Sister   There's a lot of bitterness there

Harry   Dont I have the right to be bitter ?

Sister   No

Harry   How would you know ? You've never been here

Sister   I have, Mr Moss, I 've been to the door many
          times

Harry   But never gone through...

          (She turns to go)

          Sister... can I ask you something ?

Sister   Ask away

Harry   Will you be honest with me ?

Sister   In what way ?

Harry   I want to know - as it happens - I want to
          know what to expect next

Sister   We dont normally -

Harry   I know you dont, but you could make an
          exception - for me

Sister   I'll speak to the doctor

Harry   Is there much pain ?

Sister   We try to keep that to a minimum

Harry	Not that I'm afraid of it you understand – I just want to know what to expect
Sister	I'll try and keep you fully informed
Harry	Scouts honour ?
Sister	(Saluting like scout) Scouts honour

(<u>Scene change</u> – blackout with music – the lights rise to find Harry in dressing gown and pyjamas sitting on a bench in the garden writing in his diary, Behind the birdsong there is a mixture of distant traffic and teenage girls laughing nearby whilst playing an outdoor game))

Harry	(Either voice-over or as he writes) Its ages since I kept a diary – not since I was a child – never seen the reason for it till now ....Why am I writing this ? To put things into perspective, to get things into place – perhaps someone will read it after I've gone – someone may benefit – I hope so – "He gave his life" and all that... the place is quite nice really, if you like that sort of thing – everything very casual – home from home almost – only its not home – better this than being fussed over by herevery day , I couldnt stand that – they leave you pretty much to your own devices though there are the obvious hints – "Dont you <u>want</u> to join in our discussion group Mr Moss ?" – what is the point ?

Everyone has their own bit of territority, their own place, so I've claimed mine – out here in the garden where I can listen to the birds singing - I never noticed them much before

Its a nice garden, well kept, but gardening's never been one of my strong points so dont ask me to name any of the flowers.... around the house there's a wall to keep the outside world at bay or is it to keep the clients inside ? - the house must have been owned by someone very rich at one time - probably bequeathed

As I sit here I can hear the noise of the traffic going up the hill - the lorries have to change gear just a little further up - I can hear children playing and next door there must be some sort of school - a girls school by the sound of it - I never knew female laughter could be so annoying

(At this moment a plastic throwing disc comes flying to his feet. He picks it up and is about to throw it back when a girl of about sixteen dashes in - she is common, gum chewing but full of vitality)

Debbie   Sorry

Harry   Thats OK

Debbie   Bloody useless they are - can I have it back ?

Harry   Yes - yes of course

           (Gives it to her and she throws it back over the wall)

           Dont go

Debbie   Eh ?

Harry   Stay for a minute

Debbie   You what ?

Harry   Sit down - have a cigarette or something

Debbie   Whats this place ? An'ospital or something ?

Harry   Yes - a hospital - I've not got anything
           catching though

Debbie   Doesnt bother me if you have - we've all got
           to go sometime havent we ?

           (They sit on the bench - he offers her a
           cigarette and lights it for her)

Debbie   What've you got ?

Harry   Nothing time wont cure

Debbie   I 'ate 'ospitals, they always smell funny

Harry   Thats the disinfectant - this one isnt bad -
           you are old enough to smoke ?

Debbie   Course I am

Harry   Only I dont want to get you into any kind of
           trouble

           (She laughs)

           Whats so funny ?

Debbie   If only you knew

Harry	Whát've I said ?
Debbie	Nothing
Harry	(Indicating where shes come from) That place what is it ? - A school ?
Debbie	Nah - its an 'ostel
Harry	A hostel ?
Debbie	Probation 'ostel
Harry	Oh, so you've been in trouble already ?
Debbie	You might say - I aint been done for smoking under age though
Harry	What are you in for ?
Debbie	Nicking - what about you ?
Harry	Life... what did you nick - I mean steal ?
Debbie	Just some gear from a shop
Harry	That sounds a bit steep, putting you in a hostel for shoplifting
Debbie	It werent the first time - its while they do reports on you
Harry	What did your parents say ?
Debbie	Not a lot - been in care since I was eight
Harry	Oh, I'm sorry
Debbie	Nothing to be sorry about

Harry	So how long do you have to stay in the hostel ?
Debbie	Till the court case - you've got to keep your nose clean for a couple of weeks then back to court for sentencing
Harry	What'll they do with you ?
Debbie	Not much they can do - they dont like locking girls up see - 'ere, why am I telling you all this ?
Harry	Because I asked
Debbie	You're not a copper are you ?
Harry	No
Debbie	What do you do then when you're not in 'ere ?
Harry	I'm - I used to be a teacher
Debbie	A teacher ? I hate teachers
Harry	Really ?
Debbie	Not all of them - you do get some nice ones - what do you teach ?
Harry	English - Drama
Debbie	Thats not so bad then - as long as its not maths or science - I cant stand maths
Harry	Which school do you go to ?
Debbie	I dont - I got expelled

Harry	For nicking ?
Debbie	Fighting
Harry	You're quite a girl arent you ?
Debbie	You taking the piss ?
Harry	No, not at all - what else have you been in trouble for ?
Debbie	You name it, I've done it - burglary - TWOC -
Harry	Whats TWOC ?
Debbie	Taking without the owners consent
Harry	Oh I see
Debbie	Assault - robbery -
Harry	You have been busy
Debbie	Stupid really, never again
Harry	Going straight now are you ?
Debbie	I didnt say that - I wont get caught next time
Harry	Can I ask you something ? Dont you ever feel any remorse taking things that dont belong to you ?
Debbie	Come off it - you're talking like a vicar
Harry	No, I'm interested - when you take something from a shop, say, doesnt it bother you ?

Debbie	Why should it ?
Harry	Its not yours to take
Debbie	It is after I've taken it
Harry	But its illegal, its wrong
Debbie	It might be to you - what do you want me to do ?
Harry	You're supposed to pay for what you take
Debbie	You mean get a job, join the system ? Nah, tried it once - stacking shelves - not worth the hassle
Harry	Dont you want to go straight ?
Debbie	Its harder than you think... anyway I'd better be going
Harry	Will you -
Debbie	What ?
Harry	Will you come again another day - for a chat ?
Debbie	I dont know - I just about done myself in on that wall
Harry	I'd appreciate it
Debbie	I'll think about it - see you
	(She is gone as quickly as she came)
Sister	(Coming in with a tray) Who was that ?

Harry	Just some girl from next door
Sister	I hope you werent encouraging her - they can be an awful nuisance
Harry	She was all right - quite refreshing really

(<u>Scene change</u> Harry's bedroom at night where he sits writing his diary)

Harry	The strangest thing happened - there I was sitting in the garden feeling very sorry for myself when this - this nymphette appeared over the wall - she's a girl from the probation hostel next door - a bit common really but interesting nevertheless - a very unusual young lady...what interested me was her complete disregard for all social values - she doesnt seem to give a damn for anyone else except herself - unlike Moira who's constantly worrying about the starving millions in deprived countries and doing bugger all about it...talking to her was like a breath of fresh air - I dont know if she'll come again - I hope so - I asked her to...

(<u>scene change</u> - lights fade and return to morning in Harry's bedroom where Moira is doing one of her welfare visits)

Moira	(Unloading bag)...And I made you some cakes in case you feel peckish
Harry	Moira, the food in here is quite sufficient, theres no need to go to all this trouble
Moira	Its no trouble - and a chap from your school came round with this (produces card in envelope)

- 18 -

Harry	What is it ? Oh God ! A get well card - dont they know I'm not going to get well soon - the prats
Moira	You never know Harry, miracles do happen
Harry	Do they ?
Moira	Its been signed by everyone - they're all very concerned
Harry	Which is more than they were when I worked amongst them... (he reads card) Whats this ? "Chin up - Mike Benson" - that bastard cant wait for me to snuff it so he can have my job
Moira	Dont Harry
Harry	Why not ? Its true
Moira	And I brought you some books to read
Harry	Not long ones are they ? "Gardening for beginners" - great - and "How to get your point across in thirty seconds or less" - well that should be very useful when I meet Saint Peter at the pearly gates !
Moira	Have you got everything you need ?
Harry	Yes - everythings hunky-dory
Moira	Only I didnt know what I might have forgotten
Harry	You havent forgotten anything Moira, you've thought of everything - you feed my body but not my soul
Moira	I dont know what you mean

Harry	No, love
Moira	Have you made any friends ?
Harry	No
Moira	No ?
Harry	Why should I ? They're not going to be lasting ones ... what would we have to talk about ? "Oh you've got six months left have you ? I've got eight " - yes, we'll have a lot in common
Moira	Theres no need to be sarcastic
Harry	Have you any idea what its like Moira watching people sitting round waiting to die ? Its not a pretty sight
Moira	Some of the others seem very cheerful
Harry	They do dont they ? I find that particularly annoying - especially the Christians amongst them - "Take me to your arms Lord, for I am ready"
Moira	Perhaps if you believed -
Harry	Dont start all that crap again !
	(Pause while she thinks of something else to say)
Moira	Are the staff all right ?
Harry	Brilliant - God knows what I'd do working in a place like this - why do they bother ? It'd drive me bananas - Sister McCluskey's the one

	you've got to watch out for - she runs the place like an army camp
Moira	Are you... are you happy here Harry ?
Harry	"Happy" ? I'm bloody delerious. Moira I'm sitting here waiting for my body to pack in and you ask am I happy - are you serious ?
Moira	You know what I mean. I want you to feel contented
Harry	I'm over the moon, never felt better
Moira	(Uncomfortable) If you dont want the cakes perhaps I'll take them to the office

(She is about to go)

Harry ?

Harry	Yes Moira?
Moira	I'm frightened
Harry	You're frightened ? How the hell do you think I feel ?
Moira	I dont know if I can cope
Harry	Cant you go to your sisters or something ?
Moira	I dont want to, they've got their own problems
Harry	I'm a problem to you am I ?
Moira	No

Harry	Well I'll soon be out of your hair and then you can collect a nice widows pension — you'll be well provided for
Moira	I dont want providing for, Harry — I want you
Harry	What for ?
Moira	What do you mean "What for ?" — you're my husband
Harry	What you really want Moira isnt a husband, its a cardboard-cut-out-man-about-the-house — to do for you and work for you — an odd job man — somebody to knock nails in now and again — you dont need me — anybody will do — as soon as I'm gone you'll find yourself another odd-job man
Moira	Thats not true
Harry	Isnt it ? You dont need me Moira — you need a husband — any one will do... I thought you said you were going ?
	(Scene change — Harry is out in the garden. Sister McCluskey is checking his pulse)
Harry	And then we moved down here... its a wonderful thing unemployment, a great social and geographical motivator — either you look for work or you starve — they've got you by the short and curlies.. do you realise it wasnt till people like Arkwright invented the Spinning Jenny that the population became enslaved — until then everyone did their own thing, worked in their own homes and then industrialisation meant they all had to join the rat race, travel to the factory each day

Sister	But not you - you trained to be a teacher
Harry	I was still enslaved, make no bones about it - teachers go to the factory each day only its a different type of product they turn out - I used to stand in front of that class and think to myself "Here we go again, another load of sausages to be processed through the educational machine"
Sister	Are you a good teacher ?
Harry	Was I you mean
Sister	I mean "Are you" ?
Harry	I dont know, you'll have to ask some of my ex-pupils - I sometimes think children learn in spite of us not because of us
Sister	I'm sure you're very modest... you do a bit of writing as well dont you ?
Harry	Who told you that ?
Sister	A little bird - have you had anything published ?
Harry	Nothing worth talking about
Sister	Why dont you try writing here ?
Harry	I am, I've started a diary - but dont you dare look until... well you know what I mean... You know what ? I wanted to be an actor once but I never had the courage to give it a try - always clinging to the safe number and then when you realise what you want in life its too late

Sister	Its never too late
Harry	Isnt it ? Theres only one place I'm going from here... can I ask you something ?
Sister	Ask away
Harry	Have you ever stolen anything ?
Sister	Are you serious ?
Harry	Yes – have you ever taken anything without paying ?
Sister	I once went shopping with my parents and asked them for a packet of those chocolate coins – they wouldnt let me have them so when nobody was watching I slipped them in my pocket – when we got home they found out and gave me an awful telling off
Harry	How old were you ?
Sister	Only about five – what about you ?
Harry	No – all my life I've been an honest upright citizen
Sister	Why do you ask ?
Harry	I just wondered
	(Sister McCluskey exits, Harry returns to his paper then Debbie comes in in a temper)
Debbie	You bloody liar !
Harry	I beg your pardon ?

Debbie	Its not a bloody 'ospital its an 'ospice !
Harry	So ?
Debbie	So theres a bloody difference i'nt there ?
Harry	Yes
Debbie	Why didnt you tell me ?
Harry	There didnt seem to be any point
Debbie	You had me here under false pretences
Harry	It is a hospital of sorts
Debbie	Only no buggers going to get better
Harry	You could put it like that
Debbie	I felt a right burke, I can tell you - all my mates thought I was thick
Harry	You're not thick
Debbie	I know I'm not but thats how I felt - you should have told me
Harry	There didnt seem to be any point - what do you want me to say "Hello there, my names Harry - by the way I'm dying"
Debbie	At least it would have been honest
Harry	You're a fine one to talk about honesty... I thought you werent coming back
Debbie	I wasnt going to but when they told me about this place -

Harry	You took pity on me
Debbie	I bloody didn't - I came to tell you not to try and con me in future - I cant stand bloody liars
Harry	Thats good coming from you - anyway I didnt tell you any lies
Debbie	You didnt tell the whole truth neither
Harry	You know what that is do you ?
Debbie	Course I do and if theres any more porky pies thats it
Harry	Honour among thieves
Debbie	Anyway, how are you feeling ?
Harry	Great, never felt better
Debbie	Does it hurt ?
Harry	Only when I laugh
Debbie	What've you got ?
Harry	Nothing fashionable I'm afraid
Debbie	What does it do to you ?
Harry	It wastes you away until you cant control yourself - not very nice really
Debbie	You married ?
Harry	Yes

Debbie   Any kids ?

Harry   No

Debbie   Why not ?

Harry   We couldnt have any - probably just as well
          looking at the state I'm in... we almost had
          one once - a girl - she'd have been about
          your age

Debbie   What happened ?

Harry   She lost it - end of story

Debbie   I'm going to have loads of kids when I grow
          up, hundreds of them and a big house in the
          country

Harry   A little bit optimistic arent we ?

Debbie   You've got to be aint you - you've got to
          think positive - eat drink and be merry -

Harry   For tomorrow...

Debbie   I didnt mean that

Harry   I know what you meant

          (Pause)

Debbie   Got any ciggies ?

Harry   Yes, of course

          (Gives her a cigarette)

Debbie   They dont let us smoke in the 'ostel

Harry	I'm not supposed to either - smoking can damage your health you know !
Debbie	So can crossing the road... 'ere. is there anything you need ?
Harry	How d'you mean ?
Debbie	Anything I can get you
Harry	No, my wife sees to all that - brings me absolutely all kinds of food
Debbie	I meant ciggies or anything
Harry	You know what I'd really like ? A bloody good drink of whiskey - its ages since I had a good glass of malt
Debbie	I dont know if I can run to that
Harry	Never mind... you've not heard anything about the court case ?
Debbie	Its been adjourned till next month
Harry	It must be strange living in a home
Debbie	You get used to it
Harry	Dont you have any parents ?
Debbie	I've got a mum but I aint seen her since I got put in care - she used to argue like mad with dad then he left and we got a bit of peace
Harry	Why did she put you in care ?

Debbie   She wanted us off her hands - we cramped her
         style - then when she tried to get us back
         they wouldnt let her

Harry   And you've been in homes ever since ?.

Debbie   Of one sort or another - shunted from one
         foster parent to the next - it was my fault
         really, I was a little sod

Harry   And what are you now ?

Debbie   A big one !

Harry   You know what I would like ? Something to
         read, something more exciting than gardening
         or psychology books - can you see what you
         can find

Debbie   I'll do my best - why dont you ask your
         wife ?

Harry   Her idea of excitement is watching the paint
         dry - she's not happy unless she's decorating

Debbie   Dont you get on ?

Harry   We exist, thats all we do - we live together
         in the same house each of us in our own
         little world but it isnt a marriage, its
         cohabitation - that reminds me, have you seen
         this story about the chap with two wives ?

         (He shows her the newspaper)

Debbie   (Dully) No

Harry   Here, have a look

(Gives her the paper)

Amazing isnt it ?

Debbie   Yeah

Harry   "Yeah" - is that all you can say ? Have you
          read the bottom bit ?

Debbie   I cant read

Harry   Eh ?

Debbie   I cant read - all right ?

Harry   I'm sorry - I didnt mean to....thats all
          right, lots of people cant read, you're
          probably dyslexic

Debbie   Whats that when its at home ?

Harry   Word blindness

Debbie   All I know is I've never been able to - cant
          write neither

Harry   That must present you with one or two
          problems

Debbie   Yeah

Harry   Listen, why dont I try and teach you ?

Debbie   You what ?

Harry   To read ?

Debbie   You're wasting your time

Harry	Perhaps but it'd give me something to do
Debbie	(Nodding towards the house) What about them ?
Harry	Leave them to me
Debbie	I've always wanted to be able to - there was this programme on the tele once about a woman who wrote books and I thought "If only I could do that"
Harry	I'll have you know you're sitting next to an author
Debbie	You've had something published ?
Harry	Just one play - I dont think anybody ever performed it - I thought I was going places then, then I went through a bad patch and the well dried up
Debbie	What d'you mean ?
Harry	Writers block, the thing every writer dreads - you reach a point where nothing seems to work any more
Debbie	I'm not surprised in your state
Harry	No, it happened a long time ago
Debbie	What does your wife say about you writing ?
Harry	She was probably the reasons for it - she doesnt actually understand the process - she'll quite happily read a book but wont let you write one
Debbie	How can she stop you ?

Harry	Its a very subtle process, a wearing down – "You're not going to leave me on my own again ?" and so on
Debbie	She doesnt encourage you ?
Harry	No
Debbie	She should if you've got a talent
Harry	You dont know what its like living with a writer, the ups and downs, the moods – even I've got to admit I'm hell to live with sometimes
Debbie	I'd let you write if I was married to you
Harry	Thats very kind of you – I'll remember that next time round... did you know the Hindus believe when you die you come back as something else depending on how you've been in your present life – if you've been good you go up one and if you've been bad –
Debbie	I'll come back as a beetle then or a creepy crawlie – what would you be ?
Harry	Perhaps a blue bottle so I could annoy Moira or a passing bird to drop something from a great height
	(They laugh)
Debbie	We had this bird once that came down the chimney – there was soot everywhere – everybody was screaming and it was flapping about against the window – I went and got hold of it and took it outside and then when

	I put it down on the grass you know what happened ?
Harry	It flew away ?
Debbie	You'd think so wouldnt you but it just sat there without moving and when I went up to it I couldnt believe it – it was dead
Harry	Shock
Debbie	Something like that
Harry	There's one here that will end up like that, a one-legged blackbird – it hops around all day – dont ask me how it lost the other one
Debbie	Probably a cat
Harry	Probably – and you know what surprises me ? It never sings, never makes a sound, just hops around on its one leg
Debbie	Perhaps it cant
Harry	Or doesnt know how to – it seems such a waste of an existence – all that beauty and not making use of it...you should learn to write you know
Debbie	Why ?
Harry	The way you described that bird of yours, you're a natural writer or you could be if you put your mind to it
Debbie	Nah !
Harry	Why not ?

Debbie	You need brains to be a writer
Harry	You dont, you need sensitivity and you've got that
Debbie	You'll make me blush
Harry	Please yourself
Debbie	Do you think I could ?
Harry	I know you could - all you've got to do is apply yourself
Debbie	Will you teach me ?
Harry	How quickly do you learn ?

Harry   How quickly do you learn ?

(Scene change - music - lights up on Harry's bedroom at night as Sister McCluskey tucks him in)

Harry   We must stop meeting like this

(She continues with the bed then takes his pulse)

Has anyone ever told you you've got beautiful eyes ?

Sister   (Having none of it) Many times

Harry   Sister ? Why do you do this ?

Sister   What ?

Harry   Working here in this place - what kind of person spends their lives looking after the

terminally ill ? Are you some kind of a saint
or what ?

Sister   Do you really want to know ?

Harry   I do

Sister   Its convenient -. I could do something more
interesting but it would mean more travelling

Harry   (Laughing) And I had you down for an angel of
mercy and all the time you're just - just -

Sister   Just what ?

Harry   Human

(She smiles and leaves him to sit in bed
writing in his diary)

Harry   I had another visit today from young Debbie -
she came and sat beside me and - I dont quite
know how to say this - especially in the
knowledge that this may be read after I'm
gone - she came and sat beside me and she was
wearing this perfume, cheap perfume - I could
feel her arm touching mine through the
material, feel the warmth and ... I wanted her
- I know it sounds silly, a man old enough to
be her father and in my condition but I've
got to tell the truth - I wanted her -
physically - mentally - spiritually - all my
life I've been surrounded by young girls and
never until now have I felt the desire so
strongly - I know it sounds foolish but there
you are

Time is running short and I'm becoming
increasingly aware of the time I've wasted -

when I think of all the things I could have done with my life instead of which I did the right thing, stuck to the social rules - and where did it get me ?

I've promised to teach Debbie to read - my one last act of benificence - I dont know why I offered - yes I do - because I wanted to see her again

You must be thinking Moira "How can he do this to me ? How, at this moment in his life, can he turn away from the one who's stood by him all these years for a young girl from the hostel next door ? Do you want to know why ? I'll tell you - she's everything you arent Moira, she's young, vibrant, exciting - you dont know from one minute to the next what she's going to say or do - all this time I've resisted the temptation and now I dont know if I can...

(<u>Scene change</u> - music - Harry is in the garden when Debbie approaches)

Debbie   I've brought you a present

Harry   You shouldnt have

Debbie   Arent you going to open it ?

Harry   Of course (he does so) This reminds me of Christmas... cigarettes ! And so many - they must have cost you a bit

Debbie   Not really

Harry   You didnt... (meaning "steal them")

Debbie	What if I did ?
Harry	But that makes me a receiver of stolen goods
Debbie	If you like
Harry	I've never done anything like that before – what if somebody found out ?
Debbie	What can they do to you ?
Harry	Thats true (Then fear changes his mind) No, no I cant (he gives them back)
Debbie	What do you mean you cant ?
Harry	I cant accept them, I wouldnt sleep
Debbie	Listen, I went to a great deal of trouble getting these and now you dont want them ?
Harry	I do but you dont understand – it goes against everything I've grown up with
Debbie	I took a big risk – d'you know what it would mean if they'd caught me ?
Harry	I really appreciate it but I just cant
Debbie	(Shortly) Fair enough
Harry	I suppose you think I'm silly
Debbie	Yes
Harry	All my life I've conformed and now when I get the opportunity to break the rules I cant do it – I do appreciate the chance you took, honest

Debbie   Yeah, yeah

Harry   You'll find a use for them

           (Pause)

           What about this reading lesson ?

Debbie   What about it ?

Harry   Are you ready to start ?

Debbie   Yeah, you're wasting your time though

Harry   We'll see

           (He unfolds the paper and she comes close to
           him to read - he smells the perfume and
           pauses)

Debbie   Whats up ?

Harry   Nothing.. where shall we start ?

           (The lights fade and when they come up Moira
           has taken the place of Debbie but now she's
           at the other end of the bench reading the
           paper while Harry reads a book)

Moira   Some of the things you read in the papers - a
           person cant walk the streets today for fear
           of being attacked

Harry   Really ?

Moira   Theres a story here about a girl who was
           assaulted

Harry   You mean sexually ?

Moira	Yes - they need locking up
Harry	What happened ?
Moira	It says she got off the bus and this man followed her - he'd been on the bus watching her it seems
Harry	Yes ?
Moira	And then he walked up behind her and ...
Harry	Yes ?
Moira	He touched her
Harry	Where ?
Moira	On her private parts
Harry	Which parts ?
Debbie	What do you mean "which parts" ?
Harry	Do you mean her breasts or her vagina ?
Moira	Does it matter ?
Harry	Of course it matters - a breast isnt a vagina
Moira	They're both private... then he tried to force her to the ground but she screamed and he ran off
Harry	How sad, it was just getting interesting... tell me Moira, has anyone ever touched your private parts ?
Moira	I beg your pardon ?

Harry	Or ‘forced you to the ground ? (she looks aghast) No, maybe not – it could be arranged you know – I've still got some life left in me – How about it ?
	(He moves towards her on the bench and she moves away)
Moira	What ?
Harry	How about some unbridled passion in the herbacious borders ?
Moira	Dont be silly
Harry	I am arent I ? You dont know the meaning of the word
Moira	Theres a time and place for everything
Harry	Which in your case means eleven o'clock on a Wednesday and Saturday night immediately after the drinking chocolate ... tell me Moira, have you ever made love outdoors ?
Moira	You know we havent
Harry	I dont mean with me, I mean with anybody
Moira	Of course not
Harry	We could now if you like – its supposed to be more exciting if theres a chance of getting caught
Moira	Dont be silly Harry
Harry	Why not ? Come on

Moira	No
Harry	Why not ?
Moira	Well the grass is damp for a start
Harry	God , you're so exciting ! I dont know how I put up with it
Moira	You could catch a chill or something
Harry	Thats good coming from you. Havent you ever felt like living dangerously ?
Moira	No
Harry	Or having a fling with another man ?
Moira	Why should I ?
Harry	It would prove there was more to you than fairisle pullovers, drinking chocolate and woolly slippers... can I ask you something Moira ? Have you ever broken the law ?
Moira	Of course not - what do you think I am ?
Harry	Not even in a small way ?
Moira	No
Harry	How about sweets from a shop when you were young ?
Moira	No
Harry	Or keeping library books when they're overdue ?

Moira   No

Harry   Getting off a bus without paying ?

Moira   No - what are you trying to prove ?

Harry   I'm just wondering if theres a spark, the
           tiniest spark of non-conformity deep down
           below that conformist surface of yours or do
           you always live by the rules ?

Moira   I try to - there are some things you cant
           change

Harry   Like dying

Moira   Even that if its Gods will

Harry   Gods will my arse ! You know Moira I
           sometimes wonder what I ever saw in you

Moira   It works both ways

Harry   You meekly accept the most onerous of things
           fitting evrything in as if it all has its
           place - class distinction - nuclear warheads
           - racial discrimination - you accept them all
           as if they dont matter

Moira   Of course they matter but what can I do about
           them ?

Harry   You can stand up and be counted, make your
           views known - how else are things going to
           change if everybody just accepts them ?

Moira   "Change what you can -"

Harry	"Accept what you cant" - your father's motto - well if you ask me it was the motto of a ' defeated man
Moira	I'd rather you didnt -
Harry	Well I'm not going to fade away quietly like he did, I'm going to fight it
Moira	Harry...
Harry	Some people do - you hear these things - the power of will power - why should I accept what they say just because they've got qualifications and white coats ? They dont know everything
Moira	But you heard what they said
Harry	They might be wrong - bloody doctors ! What do they know ? Some of them dont know one end of a stethoscope from the other - sitting on their behinds all day getting fat consultants fees - I dont feel ill - all these pills they keep giving me - I dont even know why I should stay here
	(Begins to get up)
	Nurse !
Moira	What are you doing ?
Harry	I'm going to gèt dressed - sitting here all day in a dressing gown like a bloody invalid
Sister	Yes Mr Moss ?
Harry	I'm going to get dressed - call me a taxi

Sister	You cant do that - you're not well
Harry	I'm all right - I've never felt better in my life - you know what I think ? I think you've got me here under false pretences, thats what you've done... and you thought I'd just crawl into a hole and accept it - well I wont
Sister	Please Mr Moss
Harry	"Do not go gentle into that good night, Old age should burn and rave at close of day; Rage, rage against the dying of the light ... " - I'm not even old, damn it !
Sister	I think you should come and sit down
	(She approaches him)
Harry	I dont want to sit down - take your hands off me ! Bloody nurses - you're as bad as that lot in there - simple old men sitting back waiting for it to hit them - well I wont sit back - I'm getting out of here and under my own steam - you can stick your bloody hospice with its tender loving care where the monkey sticks his nuts !
	(He begins to storm up the stairs but is overcome and collapses halfway)
Moira	(Running to him) Harry !
Sister	Get the doctor - dont just stand there woman !
	(Blackout - end of Act One)

ACT TWO

(Scene : Harry's bedroom at night. He is in
bed writing his diary)

Harry   I think I must have made a bit of a fool of
myself - I didnt quite realise how weak I was
- they've told me I've got to rest and·take
things easy - they cant get much easier... I
must have passed out - all I remember is
waking up with Sister McCluskey standing over
me saying "Who's been a silly boy ?" then - I
felt as if I was a child again

I wish I was - I wish I could go back to
those happy times - not a care in the world
and everything to live for - I used to wonder
where I'd be at various times in the future -
I remember standing under a starlit sky and
looking up and wondering "Where will you be
when you're that old ?" - I never dreamed -
its probably just as well you cant see into
the future - who'd have thought I'd be lying
here listening to the sounds of the night

Its strange how sound travels at night -
downstairs I can hear the sound of the hall
clock ticking away - I used to hear one like
that at my grandmothers when I was small - it
used to be so reassuring then, like a mothers
heartbeat but now it takes on a completely
different aspect

The whole place creaks at night - cooling
down I suppose - you could almost believe in
spirits if you were that way inclined - God

knows plenty must have gone from here... and
then theres the sound of the breathing - some
nights its more laboured than others - last
night there was a lot of activity and rushing
around and this morning there was a vacant
seat at breakfast - they do it all very
casually though, very organised, no
melodramatics

I'm trying to come to terms with the fact
that the same things going to happen to me
eventually - I'd like to find the kind of
serenity some of the others have but its very
hard - sometimes I can accept it and others I
just want to scream "Why me ?" - my moods
change so rapidly... the priest came round
today - nothing too hard-sell but he brings
out the worst in me - like Moira - perhaps I
should introduce them

The wasting process seems to have started - I
lay in bed last night and went to switch out
the light but my arm refused to move - the
message was leaving the brain but wasnt
getting through - it comes and goes though

(Scene Change The lights fade and come back
to the following morning - Sister comes in
with a folding wheelchair)

Sister   Morning

Harry   Is it ?

Sister   It certainly is and a wonderful morning it is
           too

Harry   Do I **have** to get up ?

Sister	Of course you do - I've brought you a present
Harry	A bloody wheelchair ! You can sod off !
Sister	Now dont be like that
Harry	I'm not ready for a wheelchair
Sister	Of course you're not but we've got to preserve your energy
Harry	I dont use any - I do bugger all !
Sister	Come on now

(He gets reluctantly out of bed and pulls on his dressing gown)

What do I need a wheelchair for ?

(He winces with pain as he tried to stand)

Sister	Do you want me to take it back ?
Harry	Bring the bloody thing here

(He gets in)

I'll drive, all right ?

Sister	You're the boss
Harry	No, you're the boss but you have a very clever way of manipulating people

(They go to the stairlift or ramp)

Sister	Which floor would Sir like ?

Harry   Ladíes lingerie !

               (She takes him to his position in the garden.
               Across the patio is strung a row of flags for
               an open day)

Sister   Look, your one-legged friend's here already

Harry   He's looking for his breakfast

Sister   Do you want me to fetch some bread ?

Harry   I've got some

               (He pulls some bread from his dressing gown
               pocket and begins to feed the bird while she
               goes off to make his breakfast)

               Come on then - come on my beauty - here you
               are - come on boy - you dont need a
               wheelchair do you ? - you can fly away any
               time you want - one leg or no one leg - if
               only I was in your position

               (Enter Moira carrying bag of goodies)

Moira   Morning Harry

Harry   Oh... morning

Moira   (Indicating chair) The nurse told me

Harry   What do you think ? Does it suit me ?

Moira   I've brought you one or two things

Harry   I asked you a question Moira - what do you
               think of me in the chair ?

Moira	Its for the best I'm sure
Harry	I made a fool of myself
Moira	You did a bit
Harry	And now I've got to get around in this
Moira	(hesitant) Would you like me to push you round the garden ?
Harry	I'm quite capable
Moira	I dont mind, really
Harry	All right, if it makes you feel useful
	(She tentatively begins to slowly push him)
Moira	How's that ?
Harry	Fine
Moira	The garden's looking nice
Harry	It is, isnt it
Moira	It must take a lot of looking after
Harry	They have a man in
Moira	Did I tell you I've planted an apple tree at home ?
Harry	Really ? That'll be nice - how long before it fruits ?
Moira	(Unaware of what he's getting at) Two or three years they said

Harry	You know what this reminds me of ? Mother and child - pushing the pram - now I'm the baby again... thats one thing we didnt quite manage
Moira	No... do you remember when we went to Devizes ?
Harry	That was just before you lost it
Moira	Her

(pause)

	Sister McCluskey says they're having an open afternoon
Harry	Yes, theres all kinds of entertainment - dominoes, cribbage, you name it - its all there
Moira	Harry
Harry	Yes ?
Moira	I've been to see Father Connolly
Harry	Oh yes ?
Moira	He says we should talk
Harry	Does he now ?
Moira	Yes
Harry	And what would you like to talk about ?

Moira	I dont know, anything, Father Connolly says at times like this people should communicate openly
Harry	Go on then
Moira	What ?
Harry	Communicate
Moira	I'm only repeating what he said
Harry	You know what bothers me ? What I dont understand ? Why you wouldnt let me write ?
Moira	I dont understand
Harry	Dont plead ignorance, the writing, why wouldnt you let me write ?
Moira	I never stopped you
Harry	Not physically - but mentally, spiritually - you wouldnt allow me to escape
Moira	You just used to switch off
Harry	So ?
Moira	So I used to feel lonely - you dont know what its like
Harry	And you dont know what its like wanting to write - going to work each day to a job you dont want to do, knowing you've got something inside you thats trying to get out - having to subjugate it, to stifle it
Moira	I'd like to have given you a baby, Harry

Harry	And I'd like to have given the world a book or a play
Moira	Theres Sister McCluskey – I just want a word with her
	(She goes to the nurse who is arranging a vase of flowers)
Sister	Mrs Moss
Moira	How is he Sister ?
Sister	He's doing fine
Moira	No, I mean how long before... ?
Sister	We dont know that – you can never tell... how are you coping ?
Moira	I'm not sleeping very well
Sister	Thats to be expected – have you seen your own doctor ?
Moira	Yes, he's given me some tablets but I dont like taking them
Sister	Can I ask you something ? He sometimes seems so cruel to you – I cant understand ...
Moira	Why we married ? I sometimes wonder – we're such opposites – thats what everyone says – there were happy times though, before... It may have been the fact that I lost his baby – he never forgave me for that – he said he did but I know how much it hurt him
Sister	Perhaps you should talk about it

Moira	I've tried - he says I wouldnt let him write - he hates me for that - but I didnt Sister, I didnt stop him - he just used to switch off - it was as if I wasnt there - a marriage should be about sharing things - he just used to come home from work and disappear into his room - you dont know what its like
Sister	I do
Moira	You do ?
Sister	I used to be very close to someone once who was creative - a painter
Moira	What happened ?
Sister	I gave him the choice - either you choose me or the painting - he chose the painting
Moira	I'm sorry
Sister	Theres nothing to be sorry about - so you see you're not on your own
Moira	I made another cake but...
Sister	Why dont you take it round some of the others ?
	(Moira goes off to do so and the nurse comes across to Harry with a tray of drinks)
Harry	Where is she ?
Sister	She's made another cake - I suggested she takes it round the others
Harry	That'll make her happy

Sister	So could you
	(Ignoring this)
Harry	What've you got to drink ?
Sister	What would you like ?
Harry	Whiskey and lemonade
Sister	You'll have to make do with the lemonade I'm afraid
Harry	I thought as much
	(She pours him one and is about to leave)
Harry	Do you have to dash off ?
Sister	I've got things to do.
Harry	"And miles to go before I sleep"
Sister	"Stopping by woods on a snowy evening"
Harry	You know it ?
Sister	I read Frost when I was younger - a lot younger
Harry	You dont look like an appreciator of poetry
Sister	And what do they look like ?
Harry	You're...
Sister	Yes ?
Harry	I was going to say something I shouldnt

Sister	Go ahead, surprise me
Harry	You seem very distant, very cold - I thought everyone here would be very caring but - not that you're not, you understand, but you always seem as if you're holding back all the time
Sister	Very observant of you
Harry	<u>Are</u> you holding back on something ?
Sister	Mr Moss -
Harry	I have a name
Sister	Harry - if you'd worked here as long as I have you'd understand - when I started here I was very "involved", very close to the patients and then they started to... to...
Harry	"Die" is the word you're looking for
Sister	I had four funerals in my first year... and each time one of them went something of me went with them... in the end I toold myself " You cant go on like this - either you get out and do something different or you hold something back
Harry	So beneath that cold exterior -
Sister	There beats a heart of stone, Harry, a heart of stone
	(She is about to go)
Harry	Sister, I dont quite know how to say this... when my father was ill a few years ago I

tried to tell him how much I appreciated what
he'd done for me, I tried to tell him before
it was too late ... but by the time I got
round to it, it was too late - he didnt
understand what I was saying... in case the
same happens to me can I just say... you
know... "thanks for everything"

Sister   Its my job

Harry   You know what I mean

Sister   I know what you mean

(She goes quickly before her emotions show)

(Debie comes in with an exercise book and
creeps up behind Harry putting her hands over
his eyes)

Harry   What the - ? Who's that ? Debbie ?

Debbie   How did you know it was me ?

Harry   No-one else would be daft enough (Indicates
the wheelchair) What do you think then ?

Debbie   Very smart

Harry   Its got all mod cons - radial tyres - anti-
lock brakes

Debbie   What've you done to deserve this ?

Harry   Made a bit of a fool of myself I'm afraid -
had a sort of collapse

Debbie   Cant you walk ?

Harry   Yes and no - more a feeling of weakness

Debbie   Should we call off the lesson ?

Harry   No need to do that - what's that you've got ?

Debbie   Just some writing I've been doing

Harry   Let me see

Debbie   I dont know if I should - its a poem

Harry   All right then, you read it

Debbie   You wont laugh ?

Harry   Course not

Debbie   Promise

Harry   I promise

Debbie   (reading) You can take me into custody and
search me at the desk
You can take away possessions till I have
nothing left
You can lock me in a little room and question
me all day
But I have something here inside you cannot
take away
I might not have my freedom, I might not have
the key
But what I have you'll never take, the thing
inside thats me

Harry   Thats very good

Debbie   I just felt like writing it - I was thinking about what they do to you when they nick you and I felt so angry - you know what they do ?

Harry   What ?

Debbie   Say you've been nicked for shoplifting - first of all they put you in hand cuffs and march you out of the store in front of everybody else then they shove you in the car - at the station they book you in and make you take off all your personal possessions - rings, watches, jewellery, everything - they even take your shoelaces and belt in case you top yourself - so there you are holding up your jeans with one hand and then they stick you in a cell for ages till the social worker and solicitor come - they treat you like dirt - I know its wrong to nick things but they shouldnt treat you like dirt should they

Harry   No they shouldnt... so what are you going to do about it ?

Debbie   What can you do ?

Harry   You could write about it, tell the world

Debbie   I wouldnt know how

Harry   You've just done so, write some more like that - let them hear your voice

Debbie   My voice ?

Harry   Thats what writers call their message

Debbie   I dont know about that...here, do you fancy a spin round the garden ?

Harry	I've already done one lap with Moira – go on then I could do with the exercise
Debbie	What are all the flags for ?
Harry	Its open day – they're going to play lots of exciting games – dominoes, cribbage – all very sedate I'm afraid – nothing very exciting
Debbie	You want excitement ?
Harry	In this place ? You must be joking
Debbie	(Speeding up) Lets see if we can liven things up a bit
Harry	What are you doing ?
	(She begins to push him faster and faster round the garden and patio nocking things over and causing mayhem)
Harry	Hey ! Go steady ! Look out ! Yes ! Thats more like it ! Faster ! Go on, Faster !
	(Sister McCluskey and Moira appear)
Sister	Mr Moss !
Moira	Harry !
Harry	Faster, girl, faster !
Moira	Be careful Harry
Harry	What for ? In case I hurt myself ?!

(Eventually Debbie pushes him so fast that
they crash and he tumbles out of the chair
lying still for a minute)

Moira   My God ! (She runs to him) Are you all
         right ?

Harry   All right ? (Bursting with laughter) I've
         never felt better in my life

Sister   You could have killed him you silly girl

Harry   "Killed him" ! Thats good - I like that !

Moira   You ought to have more sense - are you all
         right love ?

Harry   Course I'm all right - no thanks to you

Moira   Sister who is this - this - person ?

Sister   Just one of the girls from next door -
         they're a bit of a nuisance I'm afraid

Moira   Its disgraceful - carrying on like that -
         (she tries to lift him) Come on love

Harry   Get off me !

Moira   But - ?

Harry   (Struggling on his own) I dont need your help

Debbie   Can you manage Harry ?

Harry   I just need a lift

         (Debbie helps him into the chair)

Thanks

(Moira and Debbie exchange looks)

Sister   And now young lady I think its time you were
          going

Harry   Does she have to ?

Sister   I'm afraid so - and I dont want you bothering
          Mr Moss again - do you hear ?

Debbie   I hear

Harry   No - please

Moira   I should jolly well think so - whatever next

Harry   But I'm teaching her to read

Sister   Thats as maybe but she's done quite enough
          damage for one day

          (Debbie moves off)

Harry   Debbie ?!

Debbie   See you Harry

Harry   (To Sister) You dont understand

Sister   I understand perfectly

Harry   Debbie ?!

Sister   (To Moira) I think you'd better take Mr Moss
          inside - he's had enough excitement for one
          day

Moira	Come on love - we'll make you a nice drink
Harry	(Looking back) Debbie ?! DEBBIE ?!

(<u>Scene change</u> The lights fade to show passage of time and rise to find Harry in the garden in his wheelchair feeding the blackbird)

Harry   Come on then... come on then my beauty... there you are.. I thought you'd deserted me ... she has you know, young Debbie, she's stopped coming since... not that I blame her.. nothing really worth coming for to talk to an old man who's... I am you know, old, perhaps not in years but...   .

You and me have a great deal in common, you with your one leg and me ... and they talk about Mother Nature... "Mother" indeed... what kind of mother lets this happen to her children ? ... "Its natures way" Moira would say, "Natures way - survival of the fittest"... fine if your one of the fittest

I wouldnt care if I deserved it. if I'd done something worth suffering for but I havent... honest I havent ...it just seems so unfair, so unreasonable ... thats my trouble, always looking for logic, wanting to believe in the guiding hand... I do you know, want to believe but I cant... I just cant

(Enter Moira)

Moira	Who are you talking to ?
Harry	Oh. its you
Moira	Who did you expect ?

Harry	Who do you think ?
Moira	She's a child Harry, what do you want to talk to a thing like that for ?
Harry	She's not a "thing", she's a nice girl when you get to know her
Moira	Sister McCluskey says she's from that hostel next door - that means she's been in trouble
Harry	Thats right
Moira	And you want to talk to a girl like that ?
Harry	At least she's got something to talk about
Moira	I bet
Harry	Which is more than we have
Moira	And whose fault is that ?
Harry	Its nobody's fault love, its just that we've got nothing in common
Moira	How can you say that after all these years ?
Harry	Its true - the only thing we had in common was sex and when that wore off there was nothing left
Moira	You're blaming me are you ?
Harry	I'm not blaming anybody, it just happened - it happens to lots of people
Moira	If you felt like that I dont know why you bothered to stay

Harry	Old habits die hard
Moira	Look - I'm sorry I couldnt give you a child - I'm sorry I couldnt give you evrything else you wanted
Harry	Go on - say it - "sex"
Moira	Its not my fault - I couldnt do those things - I wasnt brought up like that
Harry	No, to you "passion" is a dirty word isnt it, you're strictly a lie-back-and-think-of-England girl arent you - sex for you was something to be endured
Moira	I dont know why I bother visiting, I really dont
Harry	Because its your duty - you're very keen on people doing their duty arent you Moira ?
Moira	Do you want me to go ?
Harry	If you like
Moira	Do you know how long it takes me to get here ? Two buses it takes
Harry	And very grateful I am too - now if you dont mind...

(He begins to unfold his paper and she can bear it no longer)

Moira	You - you - BASTARD !

(She grabs the paper and begins hitting him with it)

Bastard ! Bastard ! I hate you ! I hate you !
Do you hear ?!

Harry   Oh so you do have some emotions ?

          (She breaks down and sobs at his feet)

Moira   Why do you do this to me ?

Sister   (Entering hurriedly) Mrs Moss ? Are you all
          right ?

Harry   She's fine

Sister   What have you been saying ?

Harry   Just a few home truths

Sister   (Helping her up) Come on love... (To Harry) I
          hope you're very proud of yourself

Harry   The truth sometimes hurts

Sister   Its a two-edged sword Harry, a two-edged
          sword (she helps her off)

          (Scene change - Harry's bedroom at night - he
          is in his wheelchair writing his diary)

Harry   Its over a week now since Debbie's last
          visit... surely she's not afraid of this
          lot ?...Perhaps she's ill - that could be it
          - she's as much right as anyone else to be
          ill ... I asked Sister McCluskey to call in
          at the hostel on her way to work ... she
          wasnt very keen but she agreed in the end...

          (Sister McCluskey comes in and up the stairs)

- 55 -

Harry	Did.you call ?
Sister	Yes
Harry	And ?
Sister	She's not there
Harry	What do you mean "she's not there" ?
Sister	What I say - she's been moved - probation-approved lodgings or something
Harry	I dont believe you, you're lying
Sister	I'm not, Harry, honestly I'm not
Harry	She wouldnt go - not without saying goodbye
Sister	She has
Harry	There must be some mistake
Sister	No mistake - I'm sorry
Harry	(Angrily) Its your fault !
Sister	What ?
Harry	She'd have come again if it hadnt been for you
Sister	She was upsetting you, getting you excited
Harry	Perhaps I wanted to be excited - perhaps it was the only chance I had left !
Sister	Its for the best

Harry	Its not - I liked her - she was refreshing - different - and you sent her away
Sister	I'm sorry
Harry	Its too late to be sorry
Sister	Is there something I can do ?
Harry	(Turning away) You've done enough already

(Sister McCluskey goes and Harry resumes his scribbling)

Harry   They sent her away ... the one good thing that happened to me and they sent her away... Why ? ... Why dont things go as we wish ? ..."As flies to wanton boys are we" ...she wasnt doing any harm... she had more life in her than the whole lot of them put together - and she made me want to write, she gave me a reason ... and now...now... oh whats the use !(throws the diary down)

(There's a pause then a tapping noise comes from the window... Harry is hestitant but eventually pulls himself over to open it - Debbie appears in the opening)

Debbie   Is this where the number twelve stops ?

Harry   Debbie !

Debbie   Do you mind if I come in ? Its bloody freezing out here

Harry   Come in - come in

(She clambers in)

Harry	Do yóu know what time it is ?
Debbie	Bewitching hour ?
Harry	I thought you'd gone and left me
Debbie	It wasnt my fault, they moved me - "Lets try her with one last foster family "they said
Harry	I thought -
Debbie	I know what you thought but I'm back - and just to prove it I've brought you some presents

(She hands him a parcel)

Harry	Not more cakes - I cant stand any more cakes
Debbie	Not cakes - go on - open it

(He opens it)

Debbic	You said you wanted something to read
Harry	Girlie mags !
Debbie	I thought to myself "What does a man on his own think about most ?"
Harry	Did you pay for them ?
Debbie	As a matter of fact I did ... and there's this

(She hands him another parcel which he opens)

Harry	Whiskey ! I've told you I dont want anything thats stolen

Debbie	Its not stolen, I paid for it - I've got a job
Harry	You're joking ?
Debbie	Seriously .. you'll never guess where
Harry	Where ?
Debbie	In a library !
Harry	Come off it
Debbie	Its true - you started me thinking - I thought to myself "You cant go on like this all your life girl, fighting against the system " and I was looking round for a job when I saw this advert
Harry	I dont believe it - you ? A librarian ?
Debbie	Not actually a librarian - administrative assistant - but its as good as
Harry	You'll never stick it
Debbie	I dont have to, its only while I learn to read better - then I've got other plans
Harry	Such as ?
Debbie	You know that poem I read you ? I did some more and sent it off to a magazine - they liked it and said they want to print it
Harry	Thats great - so you're a writer ?

Debbie	Seems so (Indicating bottle) Are you going to look at that all night or are you going to open it ?
Harry	Only if you'll join me
Debbie	Go on then
Harry	There's a cup over there
	(She brings two cups and he pours)
Debbie	Not too much
Harry	Eat drink and be merry - hang on,. we havent had a toast
Debbie	Heres to you
Harry	And you
Debbie	All right then - to us
Harry	To us !
	(They drink)
Harry	God, that tastes good ... who'd have thought it, you getting a job
Debbie	My probation officer couldnt beleive it either ... I'm sorry I didnt tell you I'd moved
Harry	Thats all right
Debbie	You wouldnt be bothered though anyway
Harry	I was

Debbie	Bet you werent — bet you thought "typical, she's buggered off" — how bothered were you ?
Harry	"Quite" bothered
Debbie	I would have come sooner but theres more to this working lark than meets the eye
Harry	You once told me you didnt like stacking shelves
Debbie	This is different — this is books not beans — every one of them is special — its a persons life isnt it ? — every time I put one on the shelf I think of you — have you done any more writing ?
Harry	Not much... can I have another drink ?
Debbie	Do you think you should ?
Harry	Come on — fill it up
Debbie	What about all the pills they give you ?
Harry	Bugger the pills, fill it up
	(She does so)
Debbie	So what have you been up to ?
Harry	You're joking — in here ? What is there to get up to
Debbie	Dont they ever take you out ?
Harry	Never — once you're in here mate, that's it

Debbie	What about your wife ? Doesnt she take you out ?
Harry	She can only just about cope with coming here let alone pushing a cripple outside
Debbie	I could take you
Harry	When ?
Debbie	Now if you like
Harry	Are you serious ?
Debbie	Why not ?
Harry	How would we get past the guards ?
Debbie	You leave them to me - well do you want to go or dont you ?
Harry	Bring the bottle - and that book
	(She passes him the bottle and diary then pushes him to the chairlift/ramp)
Harry	Ssssh !
	(She checks the coast is clear then quietly takes him out of the front door)
Debbie	There you go, that wasnt so difficult
Harry	I never thought I'd come out of that place alive
Debbie	What do you fancy then ? Pictures ? Restaurant ?

Harry   Its after midnight, woman

Debbie   So ?

Harry   So what I'd really like is to be out in the
          country somewhere away from this place, away
          from humanity, to smell the grass and the
          trees, away from all the bricks and mortar -
          somewhere high above everything - where I can
          get things into perspective

Debbie   And how are you going to get there ?

Harry   You can take me - in one of these cars

Debbie   You mean nick one ?

Harry   Yes - you know how

Debbie   Oh no - I've given that up Harry - I'm a good
          girl now

Harry   Go on, one more wont hurt you

Debbie   What are you trying to do to me ?

Harry   Go on

Debbie   All right then, but dont blame me if we get
          caught

          (She begins to fiddle with the lock of a
          nearby car)

Debbie   (Opening door) Come on then

          (She helps him into the passenger seat, folds
          the chair, puts it in and starts the car)

You're sure about this ?

Harry   What've I got to lose ?

Debbie   You're crackers

          (She starts up the engine, lights flash on
          the backcloth as they move)

          You O.K. ?

Harry   Yeah - great - why havent I done this
          before ?

Debbie   Because you're a conformist - thats why

Harry   Its great - (Shouts out of window) Hey ! -
          I'm a criminal !

          (The lights fade to show the passage of time
          and come up again in the countryside - dark
          sky with twinkling stars)

Debbie   Will this do ?

Harry   Yes

          (She gets out, prepares the wheelchair and
          helps him out but by now he's the worse for
          drink)

Debbie   Can you manage ?

Harry   Are you insin ... insin ...

Debbie   You're pissed

Harry   I'm pissed !

Debbie	Come on you drunken bum
Harry	I'm a drunken bum

(She pushes him to a spot overlooking the city's lights)

Debbie	How's that for a view ?
Harry	The whole city ... you know what it looks like ?
Debbie	What ?
Harry	Toytown - fairy lights - it looks so pretty from up here - I dont understand - how can it look so pretty ?
Debbie	Everything's better from a distance
Harry	You can say that again... d'you want a drink ?
Debbie	I'd better not
Harry	Why not ?
Debbie	I'm driving - I do have some principles
Harry	Tell me - if you're driving a stolen car what am I doing ?
Debbie	Aiding and abetting
Harry	"Abettor ?" - I've never been an abettor before ... you know what ? You're all right you are... nice looking as well
Debbie	You _are_ drunk

Harry	I'm not - you are nice - not "pretty, pretty" but nice
Debbie	Thanks a million

(Pause)

Harry	Debbie ?
Debbie	Yes ?
Harry	Do you believe in God ?
Debbie	I dont know - I cant say I've ever needed to
Harry	I need to - I need to like hell but I cant - why cant I Debbie ?
Debbie	Perhaps you've seen too much of the bad in the world
Harry	I've seen good as well - you're good
Debbie	With my record ? Come off it
Harry	You are - some of the worst criminals I know havent got a record - theres different kinds of crime you know - pride's a crime - power's a crime
Debbie	How can power be a crime ?
Harry	They use it, Debbie, one person over the other - the power of money, position - there's so much injustice
Debbie	You're never going to change that

(Pause)

Harry	Can you tell me something ? Can you tell me why I've lived ?
Debbie	You're rambling - you've had enough
Harry	I havent - I havent had enough - I can still remember - answer me - why have I lived ? - what have I done with my life ?
Debbie	I dont know what you've done
Harry	I've done nothing - I havent built any bridges, made any discoveries - I've done bugger all - I didnt even succeed in being a father - I'm a failure Debbie
Debbie	You're not, of course you're not
Harry	"The world should be a better place because a man has lived " - I dont know who said that but what have I done to make it a better place ? Tell me what've I done ?
Debbie	What does anybody do ? We cant all be film stars or celebrities - theres lots of people down there like you and me
Harry	But what have we done ? Its a tunnel - in one end and out the other - a bloody production line, thats all it is
Debbie	You've done good, Harry - I'm sure you have - think of all the children you've influenced, the effect you had on them - we affect people simply by living - we do - you've affected me
Harry	Have I ?

Debbie   Of course you have – you've shown me theres more to life than nicking from shops

Harry   Theres taking cars !

Debbie   This is a one-off, a special

Harry   But it all seems so pointless – we slave away, day after day, week after week and for what ? Holidays ? New cars ? They dont mean anything at the end of the day Debbie ... nothing ... you know what matters ?, whats really important ? People – respect – we dont give each other enough respect – instead of standing on fingers each day to reach the top we should be doing people the courtesy of showing them more respect ... do you understand what I'm saying

Debbie   I dont know

Harry   You must do, you do it all the time – you respect people, you didnt turn your back on me, you talked to me – not the me on the outside, the me on the inside – you made me feel wanted – relevant

Debbie   I just thought you were lonely

Harry   I was – you can be lonely you know surrounded by people – we're all so afraid of touching, of reaching out, opening up – I'm as much to blame as anyone

   (She reaches out her hand and touches his)

Harry   Will you promise me something ?

Debbie   What ?

Harry   I want you to promise me you wont change –
          you wont lose your vivacity, your love of·
          life – I couldnt bear it if I thought you
          were going to be sucked into the system like
          all the rest – you're not ordinary, you're
          different

Debbie   I'll do my best

Harry   And write – you must write – not about the
          surface things – about things that are
          important – people – justice – equality –
          promise me

Debbie   I promise

Harry   And now you can leave me

Debbie   What for ?

Harry   Just for a minute – I want to be alone – to
          be quiet – I need time to think

Debbie   I'll be in the car if you want me

          (She goes leaving him alone beneath the
          stars)

Harry   So here I am again – do you hear me ? – the
          boy that stood looking up all those years ago
          is back – I want to believe in you – I really
          do but how can I ? What kind of a God could
          do this to me ? You must have a strange sense
          of humour, thats all I can say – "Out of
          every bad there comes a good" they say – I
          wonder – what's the good out of this ? –
          Debbie ?

I must have done something to deserve it - I
must - there has to be a reason - it cant
just be an accident - it cant

So what have I done ? What have you done
Harry Moss ?... I've sinned - "Forgive me
Father for I have sinned" - thats what I'm
supposed to say isnt it ? - the set piece -
"And how have you sinned my son ?" - "You
name it Father, I've done it ...greed...
lechery..." - "Lechery my son ?" - "Yes
Father, I've had my share" - I've shown
anger, hate, prejudice - all in all a pretty
ordinary sort of existence - and that about
sums it up doesnt it - "Did you hear about
old Harry Moss ? He's snuffed it" - "Oh he
has, has he ? And what exactly did he do ?" -
"Not much, he was just an "ordinary" sort of
guy"

Well I didnt want to be ordinary, d'you
hear ? I wanted to be different, to leave a
mark, even the lowest of dogs leaves his mark
- and what have I left ? Fuck all ! A
grieving wife and a pile of baby's bones
somewhere in a cemetery - a man deserves more
than this... more than this

I'm not asking for much, a sign is all I
need, a sign to help me through, to show me
its not all one big joke - thats not asking
for much - a straw to cling to...

O.K. I've said my piece I'll be quiet now...
I'll listen... If you want to speak to me
I'll listen...

(There is the silence of the countryside at
night then the distant sound of two male

voices talking , then laughing, the laughing growing louder and louder until it echoes . demon-like around the theatre)

Harry   Debbie ! DEBBIE !

Debbie   Whats up ?

Harry   Take me back - now - take me back !

Debbie   All right, all right

(She gets him back into the car and begins driving, the lights flash behind then there is the flashing of a blue police light and its siren is heard)

Debbie   Oh God, thats all I need

Harry   What is it ?

Debbie   The fuzz

Harry   Who are they after ?

Debbie   Who do you think they're after ? What should I do ? Should I stop ?

Harry   Can you lose them ?

Debbie   I can try

(The lights change to them arriving back at the hospice having lost the police car - she takes him into the house but by now he's more drunk and singing while she tries to keep him quiet)

Harry   "Show me the way to go home
            I'm tired and I want to go to bed..."

Debbie   Be quiet - you're making enough noise -

Harry   To awaken the dead ! Yeah ! I'll be quiet - I
            will - as quiet as a mouse - as quiet as the
            grave

            (She takes him back up to his bedroom)

Debbie   (Lifting him) Come on

Harry   What are you doing ?

Debbie   Putting you to bed

Harry   "To bed, perchance to dream !" ... I've been
            a good boy Mummy - tell me I've been a good
            boy

Debbie   Yes, all right

Harry   Are you going to tuck me in ? Please tuck me
            in

Debbie   Just keep the noise down

Harry   Will you tell me a story ? A bedtime story ?

Debbie   All right then, I'll tell you a story (She
            reaches for his diary)

Harry   What are you doing ? Not from that - its
            private !

            (He snatches it off her but she sits beside
            him on the bed)

Debbie	Once upon a time there was a man, a man who was very poorly ... and one day in the garden . he met a girl from the big house next door –
Harry	You've been reading it !
Debbie	In the car, Harry, in the car
Harry	You shouldnt have done that
Debbie	You should have told me
Harry	There's nothing to tell
Debbie	Its all there Harry, every last word
Harry	Its fictitious, that isnt me
Debbie	Isnt it ? Why didnt you say ?
Harry	You wouldnt understand
Debbie	Wouldnt I ? You wanted a baby, Harry – (she lifts the bedclothes) O.K. then – I'll give you a baby (She gets in beside him)
Harry	No Debbie – you shouldnt – it isnt right
Debbie	Now's your chance Harry boy
	(Pause)
Harry	You wont believe this
Debbie	Try me
Harry	All my life I've dreamed of a moment like this and now its arrived I cant – I bloody cant !

Debbie	Its all right Harry
Harry	You dont understand – I want to with all my heart but with all the tablets and things...
Debbie	Do you want me to go ?
Harry	No – just hold me – hold me very tight ... when the time comes Debbie – at the end – I dont want to be on my own – do you understand ?
Debbie	Yes Harry, I understand
	(They lie together as the lights dim)
	(Scene change – the following morning – Harry still in bed with hangover as Sister McCluskey arrives)
Sister	Morning Harry
	(No reply)
Harry	(Mumbled) Morning
Sister	God, you look awful – you look as if you've been out on the tiles all night
Harry	I have
Sister	Wishful thinking Harry... and what shall we do today then ?
Harry	I think I'd better stay in bed – I dont feel very well
Sister	All right then (She tidies the bed) We'll just tidy you up a bit (As she straightens

the bed her foot knocks over the almost empty whiskey bottle) What on - whats this ? . Whiskey ? Where did this come from ? Have you been drinking this Harry Moss ? Have you ?

Harry   What do you think ?

Sister   Do you know what this can do to you with the drugs you're on you stupid man ? - Where did you get it from ? Your wife -

Harry   Not my wife

Sister   That girl - she brought it in didnt she ?

Harry   What if she did ?

Sister   I'd better tell the doctor

         (She rushes off only to meet Moira on the way up - they exchange words and Moira comes in)

Moira   Harry, whats this about whiskey ?

Harry   I had a little drink, thats all, just a little drink

Moira   Where did you get it ? Was it her who brought it in ?

Harry   It was, yes

Moira   You're not supposed to have alcohol, you know that

Harry   I'm not supposed to do anything I might enjoy - all my life I've lived by the rules and look where it got me

Moira   (Crying into handkerchief) What are you trying to do to me ?

Harry   I'm not doing anything to you - I just wanted to enjoy the time I had left thats all - is there anything wrong with that ? For God's sake woman stop crying , there's something I have to say to you

          (She tries to stop and listen)

          I've been a bastard to you and I know it and I want to try and apologise if I can - (She begins to speak) Dont interrupt - I know its a bit late but you asked for it sometimes - why the hell you didnt bugger off with somebody else I'll never know - I think you were right, it started when you lost the baby - I blamed you for it - dont ask me why but I did - one of the doctors said something about you having narrow hip bones and ever since then it was always on my mind

          The writing didnt help - you should have let me write - you should have let me pack in work when I wanted to - we might have starved but at least I'd have got it out of my system

          There's something I want you to promise - I want you to promise me that after I'm gone you wont sit around moping all day - I want you to find somebody else - is that clear ? None of this widow's weeds bit - all right - now you can go while I get my telling off from the doctor

          (She exits sniffling)

(<u>Scene change</u> - music - Moira comes on in outdoor coat to meet Sister McCluskey on the ground floor)

Moira   How is he ?

Sister   No better I'm afraid - he keeps mumbling about a blackbird - asking if it's singing yet - I cant think what he means

Moira   He used to feed one in the garden - it had one leg

Sister   That must be it - can I get you a drink ?

Moira   Please

Sister   I wont be long

(Moira wanders around feeling useless then Debbie comes in looking smarter than usual)

Moira   I thought they told you to stay away ?

Debbie   They did - I phoned and they said he was very weak

Moira   He doesnt need you you know - I'm his wife

Debbie   Yes

Moira   They wont let you see him

Debbie   Mrs Moss, I dont know why you're behaving like this -

Moira   Dashing about with him and bringing him whiskey - it was probably you who brought this on

Debbie	I was trying to cheer him up, to help him
Moira	And what would you know ? Have you lived with him for twenty years ? Have you ?
Debbie	No
Moira	I knew him before you were born
Debbie	I dont think you ever really knew him Mrs Moss
Moira	How dare you ? How dare you try and come between a husband and wife ? You're just a slip of a girl
Debbie	But I knew him better than you didnt I ?
Moira	Dont be ridiculous — relationships change — they develop
Debbie	And they die — the secret is knowing when to let go
Moira	I was his wife
Debbie	Why wouldnt you let him write ?
Moira	Thats not true
Debbie	Its what he says
Moira	Do you know what he wanted to do ? He wanted to give up his job — a secure job — for me to keep him while he tried to write
Debbie	Why didnt you ?

Moira	We had a house to keep up - a mortgage - I told him "You've got responsibilities, you cant just opt out" - I didnt want to be poor - do you know what its like being poor ?
Debbie	Very much so
Moira	I was brought up like that - wearing the same old dress - I wasnt going to sacrifice that for -
Debbie	So you sacrificed him
Moira	Dont talk silly
Debbie	You condemned him, Mrs Moss
Moira	You dont understand - we had a mortgage
Debbie	You could have moved to a smaller house
Moira	It wasnt just that, there were other things
Debbie	Carpets ? Curtains ? Do they bring happiness ? Do they ? You'll have them all soon Mrs Moss - the house, the carpets and the curtains - were they worth it ?
Moira	I couldnt have gone back to ... I couldnt have lived like that
Debbie	And he couldnt live without his writing
Moira	He _didnt_ write - he didnt finish anything
Debbie	He might have done
Moira	Was I to give up everything I'd worked for for a possibility

Debbie	You would have – if you'd loved him
Moira	How dare you ?! How dare you tell me I dont love my own husband
Debbie	Its true isnt it ? Well isnt it ?
	(Moira bursts into tears and Debbie leads her to a seat)
Moira	You dont understand, you're young – he wanted to do such things
Debbie	What things ?
Moira	Rude things – I wasnt brought up like that – dirty
Debbie	Sex isnt dirty Mrs Moss
Moira	It is – people dont do those sort of things
Debbie	In case they enjoy them ?
Moira	Yes – no – I dont know
Debbie	You should have talked to him, told him how you felt
Moira	I tried, I tried to explain but it was no good
Debbie	I'm sorry Mrs Moss
Moira	For him ?
Debbie	No, for you – you've got more problems than your husband

(Enter Sister McCluskey with tea tray)

Sister   Here we are - oh its you ?

Debbie   I phoned earlier - they said he was very weak

Sister   Yes - I think you'd better go

Moira   No, its all right, let her stay

Sister   Are you sure ?

Moira   Yes

           (Moira sips a little tea with the sister)

Sister   We should go up soon

Debbie   Can I - ?

Sister   I think it would be better if you stayed here
           for now

           (They go leaving Debbie below)

           (Moira approaches one side of the bed, Sister
           McCluskey the other - then Harry suddenly
           lifts himself up and shouts)

Harry   DEBBIE !

           (Debbie hears his call and goes running up
           the stairs to be with him)

Debbie   Its O.K. Harry - I'm here

           (Sister McCluskey comforts Moira as Harry
           quietly dies - it is then that Debbie turns
           away to go back down into the garden - she is

obviously saddened and goes slowly walking
alone - the rest of the lights dim - on the
lawn she sees a bundle of black feathers -
the body of the blackbird - she goes to it,
kneels down and gently picks it up and
caresses it... she is in a spotlight which
gradually grows smaller until the final sound
is that of a blackbird's melodious call...)

N. B   <u>Music copyright</u> The song "Harry" was
originally written and sung by Catherine Howe
and the right to perform this music must be
obtained on each occasion from :

The Carlin Music Corporation
14 New Burlington Street
London W1X 2LR
Tel: 071-734-3251